MznLnx

Missing Links Exam Preps

Exam Prep for

Customer Relationship Management: Integrating Marketing Strategy and Information Technology

Zikmund, McLeod & Gilbert, 1st Edition

The MznLnx Exam Prep is your link from the texbook and lecture to your exams.
The MznLnx Exam Preps are unauthorized and comprehensive reviews of your textbooks.

All material provided by MznLnx and Rico Publications (c) 2010
Textbook publishers and textbook authors do not particpate in or contribute to these reviews.

MznLnx

Rico
Publications

Exam Prep for Customer Relationship Management: Integrating Marketing Strategy and Information Technology
1st Edition
Zikmund, McLeod & Gilbert

Publisher: Raymond Houge
Assistant Editor: Michael Rouger
Text and Cover Designer: Lisa Buckner
Marketing Manager: Sara Swagger
Project Manager, Editorial Production: Jerry Emerson
Art Director: Vernon Lowerui

Product Manager: Dave Mason
Editorial Assitant: Rachel Guzmanji
Pedagogy: Debra Long
Cover Image: Jim Reed/Getty Images
Text and Cover Printer: City Printing, Inc.
Compositor: Media Mix, Inc.

(c) 2010 Rico Publications
ALL RIGHTS RESERVED. No part of this work covered by the copyright may be reproduced or used in any form or by an means--graphic, electronic, or mechanical, including photocopying, recording, taping, Web distribution, information storage, and retrieval systems, or in any other manner--without the written permission of the publisher.

For more information about our products, contact us at:
Dave.Mason@RicoPublications.com

For permission to use material from this text or product, submit a request online to:
Dave.Mason@RicoPublications.com

Printed in the United States
ISBN:

Contents

CHAPTER 1
THE NATURE OF CUSTOMER RELATIONSHIP MANAGEMENT 1

CHAPTER 2
UNDERSTANDING CUSTOMER DIFFERENCES 5

CHAPTER 3
INFORMATION TECHNOLOGY AND COLLECTING CUSTOMER DATA 11

CHAPTER 4
THE CRM DATA WAREHOUSE 15

CHAPTER 5
CUSTOMER LOYALTY 18

CHAPTER 6
CUSTOMER RETENTION STRATEGIES 22

CHAPTER 7
WINBACK AND ACQUISITION STRATEGIES 27

CHAPTER 8
SALES FORCE AUTOMATION AND AUTOMATED CUSTOMER SERVICE CENTERS 32

CHAPTER 9
THE BASICS OF DATA MINING, ONLINE ANALYTICAL PROCESSING, AND INFO PRESENTATION 37

CHAPTER 10
MEASURING CUSTOMER SATISFACTION AND LOYALTY 39

CHAPTER 11
ISSUES FOR IMPLEMENTING CRM SYSTEMS 45

ANSWER KEY 47

TO THE STUDENT

COMPREHENSIVE

The *MznLnx* Exam Prep series is designed to help you pass your exams. Editors at MznLnx review your textbooks and then prepare these practice exams to help you master the textbook material. Unlike study guides, workbooks, and practice tests provided by the texbook publisher and textbook authors, *MznLnx* gives you **all** of the material in each chapter in exam form, not just samples, so you can be sure to nail your exam.

MECHANICAL

The MznLnx Exam Prep series creates exams that will help you learn the subject matter as well as test you on your understanding. Each question is designed to help you master the concept. Just working through the exams, you gain an understanding of the subject--its a simple mechanical process that produces success.

INTEGRATED STUDY GUIDE AND REVIEW

MznLnx is not just a set of exams designed to test you, its also a comprehensive review of the subject content. Each exam question is also a review of the concept, making sure that you will get the answer correct without having to go to other sources of material. You learn as you go! Its the easiest way to pass an exam.

HUMOR

Studying can be tedious and dry. MznLnx's instructional design includes moderate humor within the exam questions on occassion, to break the tedium and revitalize the brain

Chapter 1. THE NATURE OF CUSTOMER RELATIONSHIP MANAGEMENT

1. Customer _____ consists of the processes a company uses to track and organize its contacts with its current and prospective customers. CRelationship management software is used to support these processes; information about customers and customer interactions can be entered, stored and accessed by employees in different company departments. Typical CRelationship management goals are to improve services provided to customers, and to use customer contact information for targeted marketing.
   a. Marketing
   b. Green marketing
   c. Product bundling
   d. Relationship management

2. _____ is defined by the American _____ Association as the activity, set of institutions, and processes for creating, communicating, delivering, and exchanging offerings that have value for customers, clients, partners, and society at large. The term developed from the original meaning which referred literally to going to market, as in shopping, or going to a market to sell goods or services.

   _____ practice tends to be seen as a creative industry, which includes advertising, distribution and selling.

   a. Product naming
   b. Marketing myopia
   c. Customer acquisition management
   d. Marketing

3. _____ is the ability of an individual or group to seclude themselves or information about themselves and thereby reveal themselves selectively. The boundaries and content of what is considered private differ among cultures and individuals, but share basic common themes. _____ is sometimes related to anonymity, the wish to remain unnoticed or unidentified in the public realm.
   a. 6-3-5 Brainwriting
   b. Power III
   c. Privacy
   d. 180SearchAssistant

4. In economics, business, retail, and accounting, a _____ is the value of money that has been used up to produce something, and hence is not available for use anymore. In economics, a _____ is an alternative that is given up as a result of a decision. In business, the _____ may be one of acquisition, in which case the amount of money expended to acquire it is counted as _____.
   a. Variable cost
   b. Cost
   c. Transaction cost
   d. Fixed costs

Chapter 1. THE NATURE OF CUSTOMER RELATIONSHIP MANAGEMENT

5. _____ is a method used for analyzing customer behavior and defining market segments. It is commonly used in database marketing and direct marketing and has received particular attention in retail.

_____ stands for

- Recency - When was the last order?
- Frequency - How many orders have they placed with us?
- Monetary Value - What is the value of their orders?

To create an _____ analysis, one creates categories for each attribute. For instance, the Recency attribute might be broken into three categories: customers with purchases within the last 90 days; between 91 and 365 days; and longer than 365 days.

   a. Retail loss prevention
   b. Trade credit
   c. RFM
   d. Merchant

6. _____ is defined by the Oxford English Dictionary as 'the action or practice of selling among or between established clients, markets, traders, etc.' or 'that of selling an additional product or service to an existing customer'. In practice businesses define _____ in many different ways. Elements that might influence the definition might include: the size of the business, the industry sector it operates within and the financial motivations of those required to define the term.
   a. Freebie marketing
   b. Yield management
   c. Service provider
   d. Cross-selling

7. _____ is the activity that the selling organization undertakes to reduce customer account defections. The success of this activity is when the customer account places an additional order before a 12-month period has expired. Note that ideally these orders will need to contribute similar financial amounts to the previous 12 months.
   a. Customer centricity
   b. Customer base
   c. First-mover advantage
   d. Customer retention

8. _____ or personalisation is tailoring a consumer product, electronic or written medium to a user based on personal details or characteristics they provide. More recently, it has especially been applied in the context of the World Wide Web.

Chapter 1. THE NATURE OF CUSTOMER RELATIONSHIP MANAGEMENT

Web pages are personalized based on the interests of an individual.

a. Personalization
b. Sexism,
c. Complex sale
d. Flighting

9. In marketing, customer _____, lifetime customer value (LCV), or _____ (LTV) and a new concept of 'customer life cycle management' is the present value of the future cash flows attributed to the customer relationship. Use of customer _____ as a marketing metric tends to place greater emphasis on customer service and long-term customer satisfaction, rather than on maximizing short-term sales.

Customer _____ has intuitive appeal as a marketing concept, because in theory it represents exactly how much each customer is worth in monetary terms, and therefore exactly how much a marketing department should be willing to spend to acquire each customer.

a. Lifetime value
b. Brand infiltration
c. Value chain
d. Sweepstakes

10. _____ or economic opportunity loss is the value of the next best alternative forgone as the result of making a decision. _____ analysis is an important part of a company's decision-making processes but is not treated as an actual cost in any financial statement. The next best thing that a person can engage in is referred to as the _____ of doing the best thing and ignoring the next best thing to be done.

a. Opportunity cost
b. ADTECH
c. ACNielsen
d. AMAX

11. A _____ or logistics network is the system of organizations, people, technology, activities, information and resources involved in moving a product or service from supplier to customer. _____ activities transform natural resources, raw materials and components into a finished product that is delivered to the end customer. In sophisticated _____ systems, used products may re-enter the _____ at any point where residual value is recyclable.

a. Supply chain network
b. Demand chain management
c. Purchasing
d. Supply chain

12. A personal and cultural _____ is a relative ethic _____, an assumption upon which implementation can be extrapolated. A _____ system is a set of consistent _____s and measures that is soo not true. A principle _____ is a foundation upon which other _____s and measures of integrity are based.
a. Supreme Court of the United States
b. Package-on-Package
c. Perceptual maps
d. Value

Chapter 2. UNDERSTANDING CUSTOMER DIFFERENCES

1. _____ is a method used for analyzing customer behavior and defining market segments. It is commonly used in database marketing and direct marketing and has received particular attention in retail.

   _____ stands for

   - Recency - When was the last order?
   - Frequency - How many orders have they placed with us?
   - Monetary Value - What is the value of their orders?

   To create an _____ analysis, one creates categories for each attribute. For instance, the Recency attribute might be broken into three categories: customers with purchases within the last 90 days; between 91 and 365 days; and longer than 365 days.

   a. Retail loss prevention
   b. Trade credit
   c. Merchant
   d. RFM

2. _____ is defined by the American _____ Association as the activity, set of institutions, and processes for creating, communicating, delivering, and exchanging offerings that have value for customers, clients, partners, and society at large. The term developed from the original meaning which referred literally to going to market, as in shopping, or going to a market to sell goods or services.

   _____ practice tends to be seen as a creative industry, which includes advertising, distribution and selling.

   a. Customer acquisition management
   b. Marketing myopia
   c. Product naming
   d. Marketing

3. _____ is a market coverage strategy in which a firm decides to ignore market segment differences and go after the whole market with one offer.it is type of marketing (or attempting to sell through persuasion) of a product to a wide audience. The idea is to broadcast a message that will reach the largest number of people possible. Traditionally _____ has focused on radio, television and newspapers as the medium used to reach this broad audience.

   a. Marketspace
   b. Cyberdoc
   c. Mass marketing
   d. Business-to-consumer

Chapter 2. UNDERSTANDING CUSTOMER DIFFERENCES

4. In finance, an _____ is a contract between a buyer and a seller that gives the buyer the right--but not the obligation--to buy or to sell a particular asset (the underlying asset) at a later day at an agreed price. In return for granting the _____, the seller collects a payment (the premium) from the buyer. A call _____ gives the buyer the right to buy the underlying asset; a put _____ gives the buyer of the _____ the right to sell the underlying asset.
   a. Option
   b. AMAX
   c. ACNielsen
   d. ADTECH

5. A _____ is a subgroup of people or organizations sharing one or more characteristics that cause them to have similar product and/or service needs. A true _____ meets all of the following criteria: it is distinct from other segments (different segments have different needs), it is homogeneous within the segment (exhibits common needs); it responds similarly to a market stimulus, and it can be reached by a market intervention. The term is also used when consumers with identical product and/or service needs are divided up into groups so they can be charged different amounts.
   a. Production orientation
   b. Customer insight
   c. Commercial planning
   d. Market segment

6. _____ refers to marketing strategies applied directly to a specific consumer.

Having the knowledge on the consumer preferences, there are suggested personalized products and promotions to each consumer.

The _____ is based in four main steps in order to fulfill its goals: Those stages are identify, differentiate, interact, and customize.

   a. ADTECH
   b. AMAX
   c. ACNielsen
   d. One-to-one marketing

7. _____ is a term commonly used to describe commerce transactions between businesses like the one between a manufacturer and a wholesaler or a wholesaler and a retailer i.e both the buyer and the seller are business entity. This is unlike business-to-consumers (B2C) which involve a business entity and end consumer, or business-to-government (B2G) which involve a business entity and government.

The volume of B2B transactions is much higher than the volume of B2C transactions. The primary reason for this is that in a typical supply chain there will be many B2B transactions involving subcomponent or raw materials, and only one B2C transaction, specifically sale of the finished product to the end customer.

Chapter 2. UNDERSTANDING CUSTOMER DIFFERENCES

a. Disruptive technology
b. Business-to-business
c. Social marketing
d. Customer relationship management

8. _____ describes activities of businesses serving end consumers with products and/or services.

An example of a B2C transaction would be a person buying a pair of shoes from a retailer. The transactions that led to the shoes being available for purchase, that is the purchase of the leather, laces, rubber, etc.

a. Demand generation
b. Societal marketing
c. Business-to-consumer
d. Corporate capabilities package

9. _____ is the study of the Earth and its lands, features, inhabitants, and phenomena. A literal translation would be 'to describe or write about the Earth'. The first person to use the word '_____' was Eratosthenes.

a. 6-3-5 Brainwriting
b. Power III
c. 180SearchAssistant
d. Geography

10. A _____ captures, stores, analyzes, manages, and presents data that is linked to location.

In the strictest sense, the term describes any information system that integrates, stores, edits, analyzes, shares, and displays geographic information. In a more generic sense, _____ applications are tools that allow users to create interactive queries (user created searches), analyze spatial information, edit data, maps, and present the results of all these operations.

a. 6-3-5 Brainwriting
b. Geographic information system
c. 180SearchAssistant
d. Power III

11. _____s are used in open sentences. For instance, in the formula x + 1 = 5, x is a _____ which represents an 'unknown' number. _____s are often represented by letters of the Roman alphabet, or those of other alphabets, such as Greek, and use other special symbols.

Chapter 2. UNDERSTANDING CUSTOMER DIFFERENCES

a. Book of business
b. Quantitative
c. Variable
d. Personalization

12. _____ or _____ data refers to selected population characteristics as used in government, marketing or opinion research, or the _____ profiles used in such research. Note the distinction from the term 'demography' Commonly-used _____ include race, age, income, disabilities, mobility (in terms of travel time to work or number of vehicles available), educational attainment, home ownership, employment status, and even location.

a. African Americans
b. AStore
c. Albert Einstein
d. Demographic

13. In environmental modeling and especially in hydrology, a _____ model means a model that is acceptably consistent with observed natural processes, i.e. that simulates well, for example, observed river discharge. It is a key concept of the so-called Generalized Likelihood Uncertainty Estimation (GLUE) methodology to quantify how uncertain environmental predictions are.

a. 6-3-5 Brainwriting
b. 180SearchAssistant
c. Power III
d. Behavioral

14. In marketing, customer _____, lifetime customer value (LCV), or _____ (LTV) and a new concept of 'customer life cycle management' is the present value of the future cash flows attributed to the customer relationship. Use of customer _____ as a marketing metric tends to place greater emphasis on customer service and long-term customer satisfaction, rather than on maximizing short-term sales.

Customer _____ has intuitive appeal as a marketing concept, because in theory it represents exactly how much each customer is worth in monetary terms, and therefore exactly how much a marketing department should be willing to spend to acquire each customer.

a. Value chain
b. Sweepstakes
c. Brand infiltration
d. Lifetime value

Chapter 2. UNDERSTANDING CUSTOMER DIFFERENCES

15. A personal and cultural _____ is a relative ethic _____, an assumption upon which implementation can be extrapolated. A _____ system is a set of consistent _____s and measures that is soo not true. A principle _____ is a foundation upon which other _____s and measures of integrity are based.
    a. Supreme Court of the United States
    b. Package-on-Package
    c. Perceptual maps
    d. Value

16. In probability theory and statistics, the _____ (or expectation value or mean and for continuous random variables with a density function it is the probability density -weighted integral of the possible values.

    The term '_____' can be misleading.

    a. Expected value
    b. AMAX
    c. ACNielsen
    d. ADTECH

17. _____ or personalisation is tailoring a consumer product, electronic or written medium to a user based on personal details or characteristics they provide. More recently, it has especially been applied in the context of the World Wide Web.

    Web pages are personalized based on the interests of an individual.

    a. Personalization
    b. Flighting
    c. Complex sale
    d. Sexism,

18. A _____ is a type of business entity in which partners (owners) share with each other the profits or losses of the business undertaking in which all have invested. _____s are often favored over corporations for taxation purposes, as the _____ structure does not generally incur a tax on profits before it is distributed to the partners (i.e. there is no dividend tax levied.) However, depending on the _____ structure and the jurisdiction in which it operates, owners of a _____ may be exposed to greater personal liability than they would as shareholders of a corporation.
    a. Partnership
    b. Brand piracy
    c. Fair Debt Collection Practices Act
    d. Competition law

Chapter 2. UNDERSTANDING CUSTOMER DIFFERENCES

19. _____ refers to the additional value of a commodity over the cost of commodities used to produce it from the previous stage of production. An example is the price of gasoline at the pump over the price of the oil in it. In national accounts used in macroeconomics, it refers to the contribution of the factors of production, i.e., land, labor, and capital goods, to raising the value of a product and corresponds to the incomes received by the owners of these factors. The factors of production provide 'services' which raise the unit price of a product (X) relative to the cost per unit of intermediate goods used up in the production of X. _____ is shared between the factors of production (capital, labor, also human capital), giving rise to issues of distribution.
    a. Deregulation
    b. Power III
    c. Consumer spending
    d. Value added

Chapter 3. INFORMATION TECHNOLOGY AND COLLECTING CUSTOMER DATA

1. _____ refer to a collection of facts usually collected as the result of experience, observation or experiment or a set of premises. This may consist of numbers, words particularly as measurements or observations of a set of variables. _____ are often viewed as a lowest level of abstraction from which information and knowledge are derived.
    a. Sample size
    b. Pearson product-moment correlation coefficient
    c. Data
    d. Mean

2. A _____ is a commercial building for storage of goods. _____s are used by manufacturers, importers, exporters, wholesalers, transport businesses, customs, etc. They are usually large plain buildings in industrial areas of cities and towns.
    a. 6-3-5 Brainwriting
    b. 180SearchAssistant
    c. Power III
    d. Warehouse

3. A _____ is a structured collection of records or data that is stored in a computer system. The structure is achieved by organizing the data according to a _____ model. The model in most common use today is the relational model.
    a. 180SearchAssistant
    b. Power III
    c. 6-3-5 Brainwriting
    d. Database

4. _____ is a method used for analyzing customer behavior and defining market segments. It is commonly used in database marketing and direct marketing and has received particular attention in retail.

   _____ stands for

   - Recency - When was the last order?
   - Frequency - How many orders have they placed with us?
   - Monetary Value - What is the value of their orders?

   To create an _____ analysis, one creates categories for each attribute. For instance, the Recency attribute might be broken into three categories: customers with purchases within the last 90 days; between 91 and 365 days; and longer than 365 days.

Chapter 3. INFORMATION TECHNOLOGY AND COLLECTING CUSTOMER DATA

a. RFM
b. Retail loss prevention
c. Merchant
d. Trade credit

5. _____ or point of service (_____ or PoS) can mean a retail shop, a checkout counter in a shop, or the location where a transaction occurs. By synecdoche _____ often refers to a _____ terminal or more generally to the hardware and software used for checkouts - the equivalent of an electronic cash register. _____ systems are used in supermarkets, restaurants, hotels, stadiums, and casinos, as well as almost any type of retail establishment.
   a. Goodyear Tire ' Rubber Company
   b. Kahala-Cold Stone
   c. Nielsen Media Research
   d. Point of sale

6. _____ is a process of gathering, modeling, and transforming data with the goal of highlighting useful information, suggesting conclusions, and supporting decision making. _____ has multiple facets and approaches, encompassing diverse techniques under a variety of names, in different business, science, and social science domains.

Data mining is a particular _____ technique that focuses on modeling and knowledge discovery for predictive rather than purely descriptive purposes.

   a. 180SearchAssistant
   b. Power III
   c. Data analysis
   d. 6-3-5 Brainwriting

7. _____ is the process of extracting hidden patterns from data. As more data is gathered, with the amount of data doubling every three years, _____ is becoming an increasingly important tool to transform this data into information. It is commonly used in a wide range of profiling practices, such as marketing, surveillance, fraud detection and scientific discovery.
   a. Structure mining
   b. Power III
   c. 180SearchAssistant
   d. Data mining

8. _____ describes the situation when output from (or information about the result of) an event or phenomenon in the past will influence the same event/phenomenon in the present or future. When an event is part of a chain of cause-and-effect that forms a circuit or loop, then the event is said to 'feed back' into itself.

Chapter 3. INFORMATION TECHNOLOGY AND COLLECTING CUSTOMER DATA

_____ is also a synonym for:

- _____ Signal; the information about the initial event that is the basis for subsequent modification of the event.
- _____ Loop; the causal path that leads from the initial generation of the _____ signal to the subsequent modification of the event.

_____ is a mechanism, process or signal that is looped back to control a system within itself. Such a loop is called a _____ loop.

a. 180SearchAssistant
b. 6-3-5 Brainwriting
c. Power III
d. Feedback

9. _____ is defined by the American _____ Association as the activity, set of institutions, and processes for creating, communicating, delivering, and exchanging offerings that have value for customers, clients, partners, and society at large. The term developed from the original meaning which referred literally to going to market, as in shopping, or going to a market to sell goods or services.

_____ practice tends to be seen as a creative industry, which includes advertising, distribution and selling.

a. Marketing
b. Customer acquisition management
c. Marketing myopia
d. Product naming

10. In economics, an externality or spillover of an economic transaction is an impact on a party that is not directly involved in the transaction. In such a case, prices do not reflect the full costs or benefits in production or consumption of a product or service. A positive impact is called an _____ benefit, while a negative impact is called an _____ cost.
a. AMAX
b. External
c. ACNielsen
d. ADTECH

11. _____ , according to Cornish, 'the process of acquiring and analyzing information in order to understand the market (both existing and potential customers); to determine the current and future needs and preferences, attitudes and behavior of the market; and to assess changes in the business environment that may affect the size and nature of the market in the future.' ('Product', 1997, p147.)

Chapter 3. INFORMATION TECHNOLOGY AND COLLECTING CUSTOMER DATA

This figure shows how the interaction between variables from producers, communication channels, and consumers vary the effectiveness of _____ which affects the performance of the sales of a new product. The product is central in a circle because it helps to direct what information is gathered and how.

a. Brand parity
b. Co-branding
c. Line extension
d. Market intelligence

12. A supply chain is the system of organizations, people, technology, activities, information and resources involved in moving a product or service from _____ to customer. Supply chain activities transform natural resources, raw materials and components into a finished product that is delivered to the end customer. In sophisticated supply chain systems, used products may re-enter the supply chain at any point where residual value is recyclable.
a. Bringin' Home the Oil
b. Rebate
c. Supplier
d. Product line extension

Chapter 4. THE CRM DATA WAREHOUSE

1. _____ refer to a collection of facts usually collected as the result of experience, observation or experiment or a set of premises. This may consist of numbers, words particularly as measurements or observations of a set of variables. _____ are often viewed as a lowest level of abstraction from which information and knowledge are derived.
   a. Sample size
   b. Mean
   c. Pearson product-moment correlation coefficient
   d. Data

2. A _____ is a commercial building for storage of goods. _____s are used by manufacturers, importers, exporters, wholesalers, transport businesses, customs, etc. They are usually large plain buildings in industrial areas of cities and towns.
   a. 6-3-5 Brainwriting
   b. Power III
   c. Warehouse
   d. 180SearchAssistant

3. _____ is a method used for analyzing customer behavior and defining market segments. It is commonly used in database marketing and direct marketing and has received particular attention in retail.

   _____ stands for

   - Recency - When was the last order?
   - Frequency - How many orders have they placed with us?
   - Monetary Value - What is the value of their orders?

   To create an _____ analysis, one creates categories for each attribute. For instance, the Recency attribute might be broken into three categories: customers with purchases within the last 90 days; between 91 and 365 days; and longer than 365 days.

   a. Merchant
   b. Retail loss prevention
   c. Trade credit
   d. RFM

4. _____ or _____ data refers to selected population characteristics as used in government, marketing or opinion research, or the _____ profiles used in such research. Note the distinction from the term 'demography' Commonly-used _____ include race, age, income, disabilities, mobility (in terms of travel time to work or number of vehicles available), educational attainment, home ownership, employment status, and even location.

Chapter 4. THE CRM DATA WAREHOUSE

   a. Albert Einstein
   b. African Americans
   c. AStore
   d. Demographic

5. _____ refers to selected population characteristics as used in government, marketing or opinion research, or the demographic profiles used in such research. Note the distinction from the term 'demography' Commonly-used demographics include race, age, income, disabilities, mobility (in terms of travel time to work or number of vehicles available), educational attainment, home ownership, employment status, and even location.
   a. AStore
   b. Demographic data
   c. Albert Einstein
   d. African Americans

6. _____ is the study of the Earth and its lands, features, inhabitants, and phenomena. A literal translation would be 'to describe or write about the Earth'. The first person to use the word '_____' was Eratosthenes .
   a. Geography
   b. Power III
   c. 6-3-5 Brainwriting
   d. 180SearchAssistant

7. In environmental modeling and especially in hydrology, a _____ model means a model that is acceptably consistent with observed natural processes, i.e. that simulates well, for example, observed river discharge. It is a key concept of the so-called Generalized Likelihood Uncertainty Estimation (GLUE) methodology to quantify how uncertain environmental predictions are.
   a. Power III
   b. Behavioral
   c. 180SearchAssistant
   d. 6-3-5 Brainwriting

8. A _____ in programming languages is an attribute of a data which tells the computer (and the programmer) something about the kind of data it is. This involves setting constraints on the datum, such as what values it can take and what operations may be performed upon it.

In a broad sense, a _____ defines a set of values and the allowable operations on those values.

a. 180SearchAssistant
b. Power III
c. Data type
d. 6-3-5 Brainwriting

9. In the field of marketing, demographics, opinion research, and social research in general, _____ variables are any attributes relating to personality, values, attitudes, interests, or lifestyles. They are also called IAO variables . They can be contrasted with demographic variables (such as age and gender), behavioral variables (such as usage rate or loyalty), and bizographic variables (such as industry, seniority and functional area.)
   a. Lifetime value
   b. Marketing myopia
   c. Business-to-business
   d. Psychographic

Chapter 5. CUSTOMER LOYALTY

1. The loyalty business model is a business model used in strategic management in which company resources are employed so as to increase the loyalty of customers and other stakeholders in the expectation that corporate objectives will be met or surpassed. A typical example of this type of model is: quality of product or service leads to customer satisfaction, which leads to _____, which leads to profitability.

Fredrick Reichheld (1996) expanded the loyalty business model beyond customers and employees.

   a. 180SearchAssistant
   b. Power III
   c. 6-3-5 Brainwriting
   d. Customer loyalty

2. _____ is a method used for analyzing customer behavior and defining market segments. It is commonly used in database marketing and direct marketing and has received particular attention in retail.

_____ stands for

   - Recency - When was the last order?
   - Frequency - How many orders have they placed with us?
   - Monetary Value - What is the value of their orders?

To create an _____ analysis, one creates categories for each attribute. For instance, the Recency attribute might be broken into three categories: customers with purchases within the last 90 days; between 91 and 365 days; and longer than 365 days.

   a. Trade credit
   b. Merchant
   c. Retail loss prevention
   d. RFM

3. In environmental modeling and especially in hydrology, a _____ model means a model that is acceptably consistent with observed natural processes, i.e. that simulates well, for example, observed river discharge. It is a key concept of the so-called Generalized Likelihood Uncertainty Estimation (GLUE) methodology to quantify how uncertain environmental predictions are.
   a. Power III
   b. 6-3-5 Brainwriting
   c. Behavioral
   d. 180SearchAssistant

4. A _____ is a collection of symbols, experiences and associations connected with a product, a service, a person or any other artifact or entity.

Chapter 5. CUSTOMER LOYALTY

_____s have become increasingly important components of culture and the economy, now being described as 'cultural accessories and personal philosophies'.

Some people distinguish the psychological aspect of a _____ from the experiential aspect.

a. Brand
b. Store brand
c. Brand equity
d. Brandable software

5. _____, in marketing, consists of a consumer's commitment to repurchase the brand and can be demonstrated by repeated buying of a product or service or other positive behaviors such as word of mouth advocacy. True _____ implies that the consumer is willing, at least on occasion, to put aside their own desires in the interest of the brand. _____ has been proclaimed by some to be the ultimate goal of marketing.

a. Brand awareness
b. Brand implementation
c. Trade Symbols
d. Brand loyalty

6. _____, a business term, is a measure of how products and services supplied by a company meet or surpass customer expectation. It is seen as a key performance indicator within business and is part of the four perspectives of a Balanced Scorecard.

In a competitive marketplace where businesses compete for customers, _____ is seen as a key differentiator and increasingly has become a key element of business strategy.

a. Customer base
b. Supplier diversity
c. Psychological pricing
d. Customer satisfaction

7. _____ refers to the marketing effects or outcomes that accrue to a product with its brand name compared with those that would accrue if the same product did not have the brand name . And, at the root of these marketing effects is consumers' knowledge. In other words, consumers' knowledge about a brand makes manufacturers/advertisers respond differently or adopt appropriately adapt measures for the marketing of the brand .

a. Product extension
b. Brand equity
c. Brand image
d. Brand aversion

8. _____ refer to a collection of facts usually collected as the result of experience, observation or experiment or a set of premises. This may consist of numbers, words particularly as measurements or observations of a set of variables. _____ are often viewed as a lowest level of abstraction from which information and knowledge are derived.
a. Mean
b. Sample size
c. Pearson product-moment correlation coefficient
d. Data

9. A _____ refers to how a corporation is perceived. It is a generally accepted image of what a company 'stands for'. The creation of a _____ is an exercise in perception management.
a. Corporate image
b. Demand generation
c. Lifetime value
d. Buying center

10. In finance, an _____ is a contract between a buyer and a seller that gives the buyer the right--but not the obligation-- to buy or to sell a particular asset (the underlying asset) at a later day at an agreed price. In return for granting the _____, the seller collects a payment (the premium) from the buyer. A call _____ gives the buyer the right to buy the underlying asset; a put _____ gives the buyer of the _____ the right to sell the underlying asset.
a. AMAX
b. ACNielsen
c. Option
d. ADTECH

11. Competitiveness is a comparative concept of the ability and performance of a firm, sub-sector or country to sell and supply goods and/or services in a given market. Although widely used in economics and business management, the usefulness of the concept, particularly in the context of national competitiveness, is vigorously disputed by economists, such as Paul Krugman .

The term may also be applied to markets, where it is used to refer to the extent to which the market structure may be regarded as perfectly _____.

a. Geographical pricing
b. Competitive
c. Free trade zone
d. Customs union

12. _____ in economics and business is the result of an exchange and from that trade we assign a numerical monetary value to a good, service or asset. If I trade 4 apples for an orange, the _____ of an orange is 4 - apples. Inversely, the _____ of an apple is 1/4 oranges.
a. Contribution margin-based pricing
b. Pricing
c. Discounts and allowances
d. Price

Chapter 6. CUSTOMER RETENTION STRATEGIES

1. In economics and sociology, an _____ is any factor (financial or non-financial) that enables or motivates a particular course of action, or counts as a reason for preferring one choice to the alternatives. It is an expectation that encourages people to behave in a certain way. Since human beings are purposeful creatures, the study of _____ structures is central to the study of all economic activity (both in terms of individual decision-making and in terms of co-operation and competition within a larger institutional structure.)

   a. AMAX
   b. Incentive
   c. ACNielsen
   d. ADTECH

2. _____ is defined by the American _____ Association as the activity, set of institutions, and processes for creating, communicating, delivering, and exchanging offerings that have value for customers, clients, partners, and society at large. The term developed from the original meaning which referred literally to going to market, as in shopping, or going to a market to sell goods or services.

   _____ practice tends to be seen as a creative industry, which includes advertising, distribution and selling.

   a. Customer acquisition management
   b. Product naming
   c. Marketing myopia
   d. Marketing

3. _____ is a form of marketing developed from direct response marketing campaigns conducted in the 1970's and 1980's which emphasizes customer retention and satisfaction, rather than a dominant focus on 'point of sale' transactions.

   _____ differs from other forms of marketing in that it recognizes the long term value to the firm of keeping customers, as opposed to direct or 'Intrusion' marketing, which focuses upon acquisition of new clients by targeting majority demographics based upon prospective client lists.

   _____ refers to long-term and mutually beneficial arrangement wherein both buyer and seller focus on value enhancement through the certain of more satisfying exchange. This approach attempts to transcend the simple purchase exchange process with customer to make more meaningful and richer contact by providing a more holistic, personalized purchase, and use orn consumption experience to create stronger ties.

   a. Relationship marketing
   b. Diversity marketing
   c. Global marketing
   d. Guerrilla Marketing

4. _____ is a method used for analyzing customer behavior and defining market segments. It is commonly used in database marketing and direct marketing and has received particular attention in retail.

Chapter 6. CUSTOMER RETENTION STRATEGIES

_____ stands for

- Recency - When was the last order?
- Frequency - How many orders have they placed with us?
- Monetary Value - What is the value of their orders?

To create an _____ analysis, one creates categories for each attribute. For instance, the Recency attribute might be broken into three categories: customers with purchases within the last 90 days; between 91 and 365 days; and longer than 365 days.

a. Merchant
b. RFM
c. Retail loss prevention
d. Trade credit

5. _____ refer to a collection of facts usually collected as the result of experience, observation or experiment or a set of premises. This may consist of numbers, words particularly as measurements or observations of a set of variables. _____ are often viewed as a lowest level of abstraction from which information and knowledge are derived.

a. Mean
b. Sample size
c. Pearson product-moment correlation coefficient
d. Data

6. Cognition is the scientific term for 'the process of thought.' Its usage varies in different ways in accord with different disciplines: For example, in psychology and _____ science it refers to an information processing view of an individual's psychological functions. Other interpretations of the meaning of cognition link it to the development of concepts; individual minds, groups, organizations, and even larger coalitions of entities, can be modelled as 'societies' (Society of Mind), which cooperate to form concepts.

The autonomous elements of each 'society' would have the opportunity to demonstrate emergent behavior in the face of some crisis or opportunity.

a. 6-3-5 Brainwriting
b. 180SearchAssistant
c. Power III
d. Cognitive

Chapter 6. CUSTOMER RETENTION STRATEGIES

7. _____ is an uncomfortable feeling caused by holding two contradictory ideas simultaneously. The 'ideas' or 'cognitions' in question may include attitudes and beliefs, and also the awareness of one's behavior. The theory of _____ proposes that people have a motivational drive to reduce dissonance by changing their attitudes, beliefs, and behaviors, or by justifying or rationalizing their attitudes, beliefs, and behaviors.
   a. Perception
   b. 180SearchAssistant
   c. Cognitive dissonance
   d. Power III

8. A _____ is a plan of action designed to achieve a particular goal.

   _____ is different from tactics. In military terms, tactics is concerned with the conduct of an engagement while _____ is concerned with how different engagements are linked.

   a. Power III
   b. 180SearchAssistant
   c. 6-3-5 Brainwriting
   d. Strategy

9. _____ is an ongoing process that occurs strictly within a company or organization whereby the functional process aligns, motivates and empowers employees at all management levels to consistently deliver a satisfying customer experience. According to Burkitt and Zealley, 'the challenge for _____ is not only to get the right messages across, but to embed them in such a way that they both change and reinforce employee behaviour'.
   a. ADTECH
   b. ACNielsen
   c. AMAX
   d. Internal marketing

10. _____ or personalisation is tailoring a consumer product, electronic or written medium to a user based on personal details or characteristics they provide. More recently, it has especially been applied in the context of the World Wide Web.

    Web pages are personalized based on the interests of an individual.

    a. Flighting
    b. Complex sale
    c. Sexism,
    d. Personalization

Chapter 6. CUSTOMER RETENTION STRATEGIES

11. A _____ is a type of business entity in which partners (owners) share with each other the profits or losses of the business undertaking in which all have invested. _____s are often favored over corporations for taxation purposes, as the _____ structure does not generally incur a tax on profits before it is distributed to the partners (i.e. there is no dividend tax levied.) However, depending on the _____ structure and the jurisdiction in which it operates, owners of a _____ may be exposed to greater personal liability than they would as shareholders of a corporation.

   a. Fair Debt Collection Practices Act
   b. Competition law
   c. Brand piracy
   d. Partnership

12. _____ is a social psychology theory developed by Fritz Heider, Harold Kelley, Edward E. Jones, and Lee Ross.

The theory is concerned with the ways in which people explain (or attribute) the behavior of others or themselves (self-attribution) with something else. It explores how individuals 'attribute' causes to events and how this cognitive perception affects their usefulness in an organization.

   a. AMAX
   b. ACNielsen
   c. ADTECH
   d. Attribution theory

13. Mystery shopping or Mystery Consumer is a tool used by market research companies to measure quality of retail service or gather specific information about products and services. _____ posing as normal customers perform specific tasks-- such as purchasing a product, asking questions, registering complaints or behaving in a certain way - and then provide detailed reports or feedback about their experiences.

Mystery shopping began in the 1940s as a way to measure employee integrity.

   a. Questionnaire
   b. Mystery shopping
   c. Market research
   d. Mystery shoppers

14. In psychology, philosophy, and the cognitive sciences, _____ is the process of attaining awareness or understanding of sensory information. It is a task far more complex than was imagined in the 1950s and 1960s, when it was predicted that building perceiving machines would take about a decade, a goal which is still very far from fruition. The word _____ comes from the Latin words _____, percepio, meaning 'receiving, collecting, action of taking possession, apprehension with the mind or senses.'

_____ is one of the oldest fields in psychology.

a. Power III
b. Perception
c. Groupthink
d. 180SearchAssistant

Chapter 7. WINBACK AND ACQUISITION STRATEGIES

1. _____ refer to a collection of facts usually collected as the result of experience, observation or experiment or a set of premises. This may consist of numbers, words particularly as measurements or observations of a set of variables. _____ are often viewed as a lowest level of abstraction from which information and knowledge are derived.

   a. Pearson product-moment correlation coefficient
   b. Mean
   c. Sample size
   d. Data

2. _____ is a method used for analyzing customer behavior and defining market segments. It is commonly used in database marketing and direct marketing and has received particular attention in retail.

   _____ stands for

   - Recency - When was the last order?
   - Frequency - How many orders have they placed with us?
   - Monetary Value - What is the value of their orders?

   To create an _____ analysis, one creates categories for each attribute. For instance, the Recency attribute might be broken into three categories: customers with purchases within the last 90 days; between 91 and 365 days; and longer than 365 days.

   a. RFM
   b. Retail loss prevention
   c. Trade credit
   d. Merchant

3. In marketing, customer _____, lifetime customer value (LCV), or _____ (LTV) and a new concept of 'customer life cycle management' is the present value of the future cash flows attributed to the customer relationship. Use of customer _____ as a marketing metric tends to place greater emphasis on customer service and long-term customer satisfaction, rather than on maximizing short-term sales.

   Customer _____ has intuitive appeal as a marketing concept, because in theory it represents exactly how much each customer is worth in monetary terms, and therefore exactly how much a marketing department should be willing to spend to acquire each customer.

   a. Value chain
   b. Brand infiltration
   c. Lifetime value
   d. Sweepstakes

Chapter 7. WINBACK AND ACQUISITION STRATEGIES

4. A personal and cultural _____ is a relative ethic _____, an assumption upon which implementation can be extrapolated. A _____ system is a set of consistent _____s and measures that is soo not true. A principle _____ is a foundation upon which other _____s and measures of integrity are based.
   a. Supreme Court of the United States
   b. Package-on-Package
   c. Perceptual maps
   d. Value

5. A _____ is a form of qualitative research in which a group of people are asked about their attitude towards a product, service, concept, advertisement, idea, or packaging. Questions are asked in an interactive group setting where participants are free to talk with other group members.

   Ernest Dichter originated the idea of having a 'group therapy' for products and this process is what became known as a _____.

   a. Logit analysis
   b. Marketing research process
   c. Focus group
   d. Cross tabulation

6. The most important feature of a contract is that one party makes an _____ for an arrangement that another accepts. This can be called a 'concurrence of wills' or 'ad idem' (meeting of the minds) of two or more parties. The concept is somewhat contested.
   a. ADTECH
   b. AMAX
   c. ACNielsen
   d. Offer

7. _____ refers to several different marketing arrangements:

   _____ is when two companies form an alliance to work together, creating marketing synergy. As described in _____: The Science of Alliance:

   _____ is an arrangement that associates a single product or service with more than one brand name, or otherwise associates a product with someone other than the principal producer. The typical _____ agreement involves two or more companies acting in cooperation to associate any of various logos, color schemes, or brand identifiers to a specific product that is contractually designated for this purpose.

a. Target audience
b. Line extension
c. Co-branding
d. Brand Development Index

8. _____ is defined by the American _____ Association as the activity, set of institutions, and processes for creating, communicating, delivering, and exchanging offerings that have value for customers, clients, partners, and society at large. The term developed from the original meaning which referred literally to going to market, as in shopping, or going to a market to sell goods or services.

_____ practice tends to be seen as a creative industry, which includes advertising, distribution and selling.

a. Marketing
b. Product naming
c. Customer acquisition management
d. Marketing myopia

9. The _____ is a marketing concept that was first proposed as a theory to explain a pattern among successful advertising campaigns of the early 1940s. It states that such campaigns made unique propositions to the customer and that this convinced them to switch brands. The term was invented by Rosser Reeves of Ted Bates ' Company.
a. ADTECH
b. ACNielsen
c. AMAX
d. Unique selling proposition

10. _____ is a term developed by Eric von Hippel in 1986. His definition for _____ is:

1. _____s face needs that will be general in a marketplace - but face them months or years before the bulk of that marketplace encounters them, and
2. _____s are positioned to benefit significantly by obtaining a solution to those needs.

In other words: _____s are users of a product that currently experience needs still unknown to the public and who also benefit greatly if they obtain a solution to these needs.

The _____ Method is a market research tool that may be used by companies and / or individuals seeking to develop breakthrough products. _____ methodology was originally developed by Dr. Eric von Hippel of the Massachusetts Institute of Technology (MIT) and first described in the July 1986 issue of the Journal of Management Science.

a. 180SearchAssistant
b. 6-3-5 Brainwriting
c. Power III
d. Lead user

11. In economics, business, retail, and accounting, a _____ is the value of money that has been used up to produce something, and hence is not available for use anymore. In economics, a _____ is an alternative that is given up as a result of a decision. In business, the _____ may be one of acquisition, in which case the amount of money expended to acquire it is counted as _____.
a. Transaction cost
b. Variable cost
c. Cost
d. Fixed costs

12. Switching barriers or _____s are terms used in microeconomics, strategic management, and marketing to describe any impediment to a customer's changing of suppliers.

In many markets, consumers are forced to incur costs when switching from one supplier to another. These costs are called _____s and can come in many different shapes.

a. Strategic group
b. Strategic business unit
c. Chaotics
d. Switching cost

13. Cognition is the scientific term for 'the process of thought.' Its usage varies in different ways in accord with different disciplines: For example, in psychology and _____ science it refers to an information processing view of an individual's psychological functions. Other interpretations of the meaning of cognition link it to the development of concepts; individual minds, groups, organizations, and even larger coalitions of entities, can be modelled as 'societies' (Society of Mind), which cooperate to form concepts.

The autonomous elements of each 'society' would have the opportunity to demonstrate emergent behavior in the face of some crisis or opportunity.

a. 6-3-5 Brainwriting
b. Cognitive
c. Power III
d. 180SearchAssistant

14. _____ is an uncomfortable feeling caused by holding two contradictory ideas simultaneously. The 'ideas' or 'cognitions' in question may include attitudes and beliefs, and also the awareness of one's behavior. The theory of _____ proposes that people have a motivational drive to reduce dissonance by changing their attitudes, beliefs, and behaviors, or by justifying or rationalizing their attitudes, beliefs, and behaviors.
    a. Power III
    b. Perception
    c. 180SearchAssistant
    d. Cognitive dissonance

Chapter 8. SALES FORCE AUTOMATION AND AUTOMATED CUSTOMER SERVICE CENTERS

1. _____ is a method used for analyzing customer behavior and defining market segments. It is commonly used in database marketing and direct marketing and has received particular attention in retail.

   _____ stands for

   - Recency - When was the last order?
   - Frequency - How many orders have they placed with us?
   - Monetary Value - What is the value of their orders?

   To create an _____ analysis, one creates categories for each attribute. For instance, the Recency attribute might be broken into three categories: customers with purchases within the last 90 days; between 91 and 365 days; and longer than 365 days.

   a. Merchant
   b. Trade credit
   c. Retail loss prevention
   d. RFM

2. The term _____ was first coined by New York Times best selling author, Linda Richardson. _____ emphasizes customer needs and meeting those needs with solutions combining products and/or services. A consultative salesperson typically provides detailed instruction or advice on which solution best meets these needs.
   a. Lead generation
   b. Sales management
   c. Request for proposal
   d. Consultative selling

3. Sales force management systems are information systems used in marketing and management that help automate some sales and sales force management functions. They are frequently combined with a marketing information system, in which case they are often called Customer Relationship Management (CRM) systems.

   _____ Systems, typically a part of a company's customer relationship management system, is a system that automatically records all the stages in a sales process.

   a. Sales force automation
   b. 6-3-5 Brainwriting
   c. Power III
   d. 180SearchAssistant

4. A _____ is a systematic approach to selling a product or service. A growing body of published literature approaches the _____ from the point of view of an engineering discipline

Chapter 8. SALES FORCE AUTOMATION AND AUTOMATED CUSTOMER SERVICE CENTERS

Reasons for having a well thought-out _____ include seller and buyer risk management, standardized customer interaction in sales, and scalable revenue generation.

a. Request for proposal
b. Sales process
c. Lead generation
d. Sales management

5. _____ refers to a range of skills, tools, and techniques utilized to accomplish specific tasks, projects and goals. This set encompass a wide scope of activities, and these include planning, setting goals, delegation, analysis of time spent, monitoring, organizing, scheduling, and prioritizing. Initially _____ referred to just business or work activities, but eventually the term broadened to include personal activities also.
   a. Digital strategy
   b. Business plan
   c. Goal setting
   d. Time management

6. _____ is a recursive process where two or more people or organizations work together toward an intersection of common goals -- for example, an intellectual endeavor that is creative in nature--by sharing knowledge, learning and building consensus. _____ does not require leadership and can sometimes bring better results through decentralization and egalitarianism. In particular, teams that work collaboratively can obtain greater resources, recognition and reward when facing competition for finite resources._____ is also present in opposing goals exhibiting the notion of adversarial _____, though this notion is atypical of the annotation that people have given towards their understanding of _____.
   a. Collaboration
   b. 180SearchAssistant
   c. Power III
   d. 6-3-5 Brainwriting

7. _____ is the physical search for minerals, fossils, precious metals or mineral specimens, and is also known as fossicking.

_____ is synonymous in some ways with mineral exploration which is an organised, large scale and at least semi-scientific effort undertaken by mineral resource companies to find commercially viable ore deposits. To actually be considered a prospector you must become registered as a professional prospector.

Chapter 8. SALES FORCE AUTOMATION AND AUTOMATED CUSTOMER SERVICE CENTERS

   a. 180SearchAssistant
   b. 6-3-5 Brainwriting
   c. Power III
   d. Prospecting

8. _____ comprises a range of practices used in an organisation to identify, create, represent, distribute and enable adoption of insights and experiences. Such insights and experiences comprise knowledge, either embodied in individuals or embedded in organisational processes or practice. An established discipline since 1991 , _____ includes courses taught in the fields of business administration, information systems, management, and library and information sciences .
   a. Knowledge management
   b. 6-3-5 Brainwriting
   c. Power III
   d. 180SearchAssistant

9. _____ in economics and business is the result of an exchange and from that trade we assign a numerical monetary value to a good, service or asset. If I trade 4 apples for an orange, the _____ of an orange is 4 - apples. Inversely, the _____ of an apple is 1/4 oranges.
   a. Discounts and allowances
   b. Contribution margin-based pricing
   c. Pricing
   d. Price

10. In economics and sociology, an _____ is any factor (financial or non-financial) that enables or motivates a particular course of action, or counts as a reason for preferring one choice to the alternatives. It is an expectation that encourages people to behave in a certain way. Since human beings are purposeful creatures, the study of _____ structures is central to the study of all economic activity (both in terms of individual decision-making and in terms of co-operation and competition within a larger institutional structure.)
   a. ADTECH
   b. Incentive
   c. AMAX
   d. ACNielsen

11. An _____ is a formal scheme used to promote or encourage specific actions or behavior by a specific group of people during a defined period of time. _____s are particularly used in business management to motivate employees, and in sales in order to attract and retain customers.

If programs are to be effective, all the factors that affect behavior must be recognized, including: motivation, skills, recognition, an understanding of the goals, and the ability to measure progress.

Chapter 8. SALES FORCE AUTOMATION AND AUTOMATED CUSTOMER SERVICE CENTERS

a. Advertiser funded programming
b. All commodity volume
c. Incentive program
d. Electronic retailing self-regulation program

12. _____ is the provision of service to customers before, during and after a purchase.

According to Turban et al., '_____ is a series of activities designed to enhance the level of customer satisfaction - that is, the feeling that a product or service has met the customer expectation.'

Its importance varies by product, industry and customer.

a. Facing
b. Customer experience
c. COPC Inc.
d. Customer service

13. _____ is an advertisement in which a particular product specifically mentions a competitor by name for the express purpose of showing why the competitor is inferior to the product naming it.

This should not be confused with parody advertisements, where a fictional product is being advertised for the purpose of poking fun at the particular advertisement, nor should it be confused with the use of a coined brand name for the purpose of comparing the product without actually naming an actual competitor. ('Wikipedia tastes better and is less filling than the Encyclopedia Galactica.')

In the 1980s, during what has been referred to as the cola wars, soft-drink manufacturer Pepsi ran a series of advertisements where people, caught on hidden camera, in a blind taste test, chose Pepsi over rival Coca-Cola.

a. Comparative advertising
b. Cost per conversion
c. Heavy-up
d. GL-70

14. _____, known also as _____entification (Caller IDD) is a telephone service, available on POTS (Plain Old Telephone Service) lines, that transmits a caller's number to the called party's telephone equipment during the ringing signal _____ can also provide a name associated with the calling telephone number, for a higher fee. The information made available to the called party may be made visible on a telephone's own display or on a separate attached device.

Chapter 8. SALES FORCE AUTOMATION AND AUTOMATED CUSTOMER SERVICE CENTERS

    a. 6-3-5 Brainwriting
    b. Caller ID
    c. Power III
    d. 180SearchAssistant

15. _____ is one of the four elements of marketing mix. An organization or set of organizations (go-betweens) involved in the process of making a product or service available for use or consumption by a consumer or business user.

The other three parts of the marketing mix are product, pricing, and promotion.

    a. Better Living Through Chemistry
    b. Japan Advertising Photographers' Association
    c. Distribution
    d. Comparison-Shopping agent

16. _____ refer to a collection of facts usually collected as the result of experience, observation or experiment or a set of premises. This may consist of numbers, words particularly as measurements or observations of a set of variables. _____ are often viewed as a lowest level of abstraction from which information and knowledge are derived.

    a. Sample size
    b. Data
    c. Pearson product-moment correlation coefficient
    d. Mean

17. _____ is the practice of serving oneself, usually when purchasing items. Common examples include many gas stations, where the customer pumps their own gas rather than have an attendant do it (self-service gas pumping is illegal in New Jersey ' Oregon); Automatic Teller Machines (ATMs) in the banking world have also revolutionised how people withdraw and deposit funds; most American stores, where the customer uses a shopping cart in the store, placing the items they want to buy into the cart and then proceeding to the checkout counter/aisles; or at buffet-style restaurants, where the customer serves their own plate of food from a large, central selection.

_____ is used on the phone, web and email to facilitate customer service interactions using automation.

    a. Wardrobing
    b. Gruen transfer
    c. Warehouse store
    d. Self service

Chapter 9. THE BASICS OF DATA MINING, ONLINE ANALYTICAL PROCESSING, AND INFO PRESENTATION

1. _____ refer to a collection of facts usually collected as the result of experience, observation or experiment or a set of premises. This may consist of numbers, words particularly as measurements or observations of a set of variables. _____ are often viewed as a lowest level of abstraction from which information and knowledge are derived.
   a. Sample size
   b. Pearson product-moment correlation coefficient
   c. Data
   d. Mean

2. _____ is the process of extracting hidden patterns from data. As more data is gathered, with the amount of data doubling every three years, _____ is becoming an increasingly important tool to transform this data into information. It is commonly used in a wide range of profiling practices, such as marketing, surveillance, fraud detection and scientific discovery.
   a. 180SearchAssistant
   b. Power III
   c. Structure mining
   d. Data mining

3. A _____ is a list of the general tasks and responsibilities of a position. Typically, it also includes to whom the position reports, specifications such as the qualifications needed by the person in the job, salary range for the position, etc. A _____ is usually developed by conducting a job analysis, which includes examining the tasks and sequences of tasks necessary to perform the job.
   a. 6-3-5 Brainwriting
   b. Power III
   c. 180SearchAssistant
   d. Job description

4. _____ is a method used for analyzing customer behavior and defining market segments. It is commonly used in database marketing and direct marketing and has received particular attention in retail.

_____ stands for

- Recency - When was the last order?
- Frequency - How many orders have they placed with us?
- Monetary Value - What is the value of their orders?

To create an _____ analysis, one creates categories for each attribute. For instance, the Recency attribute might be broken into three categories: customers with purchases within the last 90 days; between 91 and 365 days; and longer than 365 days.

Chapter 9. THE BASICS OF DATA MINING, ONLINE ANALYTICAL PROCESSING, AND INFO PRESENTATION

a. Trade credit
b. RFM
c. Retail loss prevention
d. Merchant

5. Traditionally, the term _____ had been used to refer to a network or circuit of biological neurons. The modern usage of the term often refers to artificial _____s, which are composed of artificial neurons or nodes. Thus the term has two distinct usages:

   1. Biological _____s are made up of real biological neurons that are connected or functionally related in the peripheral nervous system or the central nervous system. In the field of neuroscience, they are often identified as groups of neurons that perform a specific physiological function in laboratory analysis.
   2. Artificial _____s are made up of interconnecting artificial neurons (programming constructs that mimic the properties of biological neurons.) Artificial _____s may either be used to gain an understanding of biological _____s, or for solving artificial intelligence problems without necessarily creating a model of a real biological system. The real, biological nervous system is highly complex and includes some features that may seem superfluous based on an understanding of artificial networks

In general a biological _____ is composed of a group or groups of chemically connected or functionally associated neurons.

a. Power III
b. 180SearchAssistant
c. Neural network
d. 6-3-5 Brainwriting

Chapter 10. MEASURING CUSTOMER SATISFACTION AND LOYALTY

1. _____ is a method used for analyzing customer behavior and defining market segments. It is commonly used in database marketing and direct marketing and has received particular attention in retail.

   _____ stands for

   - Recency - When was the last order?
   - Frequency - How many orders have they placed with us?
   - Monetary Value - What is the value of their orders?

   To create an _____ analysis, one creates categories for each attribute. For instance, the Recency attribute might be broken into three categories: customers with purchases within the last 90 days; between 91 and 365 days; and longer than 365 days.

   a. Retail loss prevention
   b. Merchant
   c. Trade credit
   d. RFM

2. A personal and cultural _____ is a relative ethic _____, an assumption upon which implementation can be extrapolated. A _____ system is a set of consistent _____s and measures that is soo not true. A principle _____ is a foundation upon which other _____s and measures of integrity are based.
   a. Supreme Court of the United States
   b. Package-on-Package
   c. Perceptual maps
   d. Value

3. _____ a research method involving the use of questionnaires and/or statistical surveys to gather data about people and their thoughts and behaviours.
   a. Survey research
   b. Z-test
   c. T-test
   d. Control chart

4. _____ describes data and characteristics about the population or phenomenon being studied. _____ answers the questions who, what, where, when and how.

   Although the data description is factual, accurate and systematic, the research cannot describe what caused a situation.

Chapter 10. MEASURING CUSTOMER SATISFACTION AND LOYALTY

   a. Two-tailed test
   b. Power III
   c. Sampling error
   d. Descriptive research

5. _____ is a type of research conducted because a problem has not been clearly defined. _____ helps determine the best research design, data collection method and selection of subjects. Given its fundamental nature, _____ often concludes that a perceived problem does not actually exist.
   a. Exploratory research
   b. IDDEA
   c. ACNielsen
   d. Intent scale translation

6. A _____ is a form of qualitative research in which a group of people are asked about their attitude towards a product, service, concept, advertisement, idea, or packaging. Questions are asked in an interactive group setting where participants are free to talk with other group members.

Ernest Dichter originated the idea of having a 'group therapy' for products and this process is what became known as a _____.

   a. Marketing research process
   b. Logit analysis
   c. Cross tabulation
   d. Focus group

7. _____ in organizations and public policy is both the organizational process of creating and maintaining a plan; and the psychological process of thinking about the activities required to create a desired goal on some scale. As such, it is a fundamental property of intelligent behavior. This thought process is essential to the creation and refinement of a plan, or integration of it with other plans, that is, it combines forecasting of developments with the preparation of scenarios of how to react to them.
   a. 6-3-5 Brainwriting
   b. Planning
   c. Power III
   d. 180SearchAssistant

8. A _____ is a research instrument consisting of a series of questions and other prompts for the purpose of gathering information from respondents. Although they are often designed for statistical analysis of the responses, this is not always the case. The _____ was invented by Sir Francis Galton.

a. Mystery shopping
b. Market research
c. Mystery shoppers
d. Questionnaire

9. _____ is that part of statistical practice concerned with the selection of individual observations intended to yield some knowledge about a population of concern, especially for the purposes of statistical inference. Each observation measures one or more properties (weight, location, etc.) of an observable entity enumerated to distinguish objects or individuals.

a. AStore
b. Sampling
c. Richard Buckminster 'Bucky' Fuller
d. Sports Marketing Group

10. _____ is a way of expressing knowledge or belief that an event will occur or has occurred. In mathematics the concept has been given an exact meaning in _____ theory, that is used extensively in such areas of study as mathematics, statistics, finance, gambling, science, and philosophy to draw conclusions about the likelihood of potential events and the underlying mechanics of complex systems.

a. Data
b. Heteroskedastic
c. Probability
d. Linear regression

11. A sample is a subject chosen from a population for investigation. A _____ is one chosen by a method involving an unpredictable component. Random sampling can also refer to taking a number of independent observations from the same probability distribution, without involving any real population.

a. 180SearchAssistant
b. Random sample
c. Selection bias
d. Power III

12. _____ is anything that is intended to save time, energy or frustration. A _____ store at a petrol station, for example, sells items that have nothing to do with gasoline/petrol, but it saves the consumer from having to go to a grocery store. '_____' is a very relative term and its meaning tends to change over time.

a. MaxDiff
b. Marketing buzz
c. Demographic profile
d. Convenience

13. _____ refer to a collection of facts usually collected as the result of experience, observation or experiment or a set of premises. This may consist of numbers, words particularly as measurements or observations of a set of variables. _____ are often viewed as a lowest level of abstraction from which information and knowledge are derived.
   a. Pearson product-moment correlation coefficient
   b. Data
   c. Mean
   d. Sample size

14. _____ is a process of gathering, modeling, and transforming data with the goal of highlighting useful information, suggesting conclusions, and supporting decision making. _____ has multiple facets and approaches, encompassing diverse techniques under a variety of names, in different business, science, and social science domains.

Data mining is a particular _____ technique that focuses on modeling and knowledge discovery for predictive rather than purely descriptive purposes.

   a. Data analysis
   b. 6-3-5 Brainwriting
   c. Power III
   d. 180SearchAssistant

15. _____ is a measure of the strength of a brand, product, service relative to competitive offerings. There is often a geographic element to the competitive landscape. In defining _____, you must see to what extent a product, brand, or firm controls a product category in a given geographic area.
   a. Discretionary spending
   b. Productivity
   c. Market dominance
   d. Market system

16. In statistics, _____ or estimation error is the error caused by observing a sample instead of the whole population.

An estimate of a quantity of interest, such as an average or percentage, will generally be subject to sample-to-sample variation. These variations in the possible sample values of a statistic can theoretically be expressed as _____s, although in practice the exact _____ is typically unknown.

Chapter 10. MEASURING CUSTOMER SATISFACTION AND LOYALTY

a. Power III
b. Two-tailed test
c. Varimax rotation
d. Sampling error

17. _____ is an advertisement in which a particular product specifically mentions a competitor by name for the express purpose of showing why the competitor is inferior to the product naming it.

This should not be confused with parody advertisements, where a fictional product is being advertised for the purpose of poking fun at the particular advertisement, nor should it be confused with the use of a coined brand name for the purpose of comparing the product without actually naming an actual competitor. ('Wikipedia tastes better and is less filling than the Encyclopedia Galactica.')

In the 1980s, during what has been referred to as the cola wars, soft-drink manufacturer Pepsi ran a series of advertisements where people, caught on hidden camera, in a blind taste test, chose Pepsi over rival Coca-Cola.

a. GL-70
b. Comparative advertising
c. Cost per conversion
d. Heavy-up

18. A _____ is a collection of symbols, experiences and associations connected with a product, a service, a person or any other artifact or entity.

_____s have become increasingly important components of culture and the economy, now being described as 'cultural accessories and personal philosophies'.

Some people distinguish the psychological aspect of a _____ from the experiential aspect.

a. Brand equity
b. Store brand
c. Brand
d. Brandable software

19. _____ refers to the marketing effects or outcomes that accrue to a product with its brand name compared with those that would accrue if the same product did not have the brand name . And, at the root of these marketing effects is consumers' knowledge. In other words, consumers' knowledge about a brand makes manufacturers/advertisers respond differently or adopt appropriately adapt measures for the marketing of the brand .

a. Brand equity
b. Brand image
c. Product extension
d. Brand aversion

20. The loyalty business model is a business model used in strategic management in which company resources are employed so as to increase the loyalty of customers and other stakeholders in the expectation that corporate objectives will be met or surpassed. A typical example of this type of model is: quality of product or service leads to customer satisfaction, which leads to _____, which leads to profitability.

Fredrick Reichheld (1996) expanded the loyalty business model beyond customers and employees.

a. Power III
b. 180SearchAssistant
c. 6-3-5 Brainwriting
d. Customer loyalty

Chapter 11. ISSUES FOR IMPLEMENTING CRM SYSTEMS

1. _____ is the realization of an application idea, model, design, specification, standard, algorithm an _____ is a realization of a technical specification or algorithm as a program, software component, or other computer system. Many _____s may exist for a given specification or standard.
   a. ACNielsen
   b. Implementation
   c. AMAX
   d. ADTECH

2. _____ is a method used for analyzing customer behavior and defining market segments. It is commonly used in database marketing and direct marketing and has received particular attention in retail.

   _____ stands for

   - Recency - When was the last order?
   - Frequency - How many orders have they placed with us?
   - Monetary Value - What is the value of their orders?

   To create an _____ analysis, one creates categories for each attribute. For instance, the Recency attribute might be broken into three categories: customers with purchases within the last 90 days; between 91 and 365 days; and longer than 365 days.

   a. Merchant
   b. RFM
   c. Retail loss prevention
   d. Trade credit

3. _____ refer to a collection of facts usually collected as the result of experience, observation or experiment or a set of premises. This may consist of numbers, words particularly as measurements or observations of a set of variables. _____ are often viewed as a lowest level of abstraction from which information and knowledge are derived.
   a. Mean
   b. Pearson product-moment correlation coefficient
   c. Sample size
   d. Data

4. Proof-of-Principle _____ This type of _____ is used to test some aspect of the intended design without attempting to exactly simulate the visual appearance, choice of materials or intended manufacturing process. Such _____s can be used to 'prove' out a potential design approach such as range of motion, mechanics, sensors, architecture, etc.

a. Prototype
b. 180SearchAssistant
c. 6-3-5 Brainwriting
d. Power III

ANSWER KEY

Chapter 1
1. d 2. d 3. c 4. b 5. c 6. d 7. d 8. a 9. a 10. a
11. d 12. d

Chapter 2
1. d 2. d 3. c 4. a 5. d 6. d 7. b 8. c 9. d 10. b
11. c 12. d 13. d 14. d 15. d 16. a 17. a 18. a 19. d

Chapter 3
1. c 2. d 3. d 4. a 5. d 6. c 7. d 8. d 9. a 10. b
11. d 12. c

Chapter 4
1. d 2. c 3. d 4. d 5. b 6. a 7. b 8. c 9. d

Chapter 5
1. d 2. d 3. c 4. a 5. d 6. d 7. b 8. d 9. a 10. c
11. b 12. d

Chapter 6
1. b 2. d 3. a 4. b 5. d 6. d 7. c 8. d 9. d 10. d
11. d 12. d 13. d 14. b

Chapter 7
1. d 2. a 3. c 4. d 5. c 6. d 7. c 8. a 9. d 10. d
11. c 12. d 13. b 14. d

Chapter 8
1. d 2. d 3. a 4. b 5. d 6. a 7. d 8. a 9. d 10. b
11. c 12. d 13. a 14. b 15. c 16. b 17. d

Chapter 9
1. c 2. d 3. d 4. b 5. c

Chapter 10
1. d 2. d 3. a 4. d 5. a 6. d 7. b 8. d 9. b 10. c
11. b 12. d 13. b 14. a 15. c 16. d 17. b 18. c 19. a 20. d

Chapter 11
1. b 2. b 3. d 4. a

www.ingramcontent.com/pod-product-compliance
Lightning Source LLC
Chambersburg PA
CBHW080744250426

43671CB00038B/2862